Industrial
Revolution
Cumulative Index

Industrial Revolution
Cumulative Index

Cumulates Indexes For:

Industrial Revolution: Almanac
Industrial Revolution: Biographies
Industrial Revolution: Primary Sources

THOMSON
— ✦ —™
GALE

Detroit • New York • San Diego • San Francisco • Cleveland • New Haven, Conn. • Waterville, Maine • London • Munich

THOMSON

GALE

Industrial Revolution Cumulative Index

Project Editor
Matthew May

Permissions
Margaret Chamberlain

Product Design
Pamela A.E. Galbreath, Michelle DiMercurio

Composition
Evi Seoud

Manufacturing
Rita Wimberley

ISBN: 0-7876-6516-9

Printed in the United States of America
10 9 8 7 6

Cumulative Index

IRA = Industrial Revolution: Almanac
IRB = Industrial Revolution: Biography
IRPS = Industrial Revolution: Primary Sources

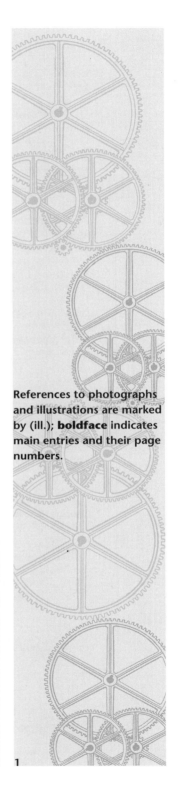

Allston, Washington *IRB:* 107

Altgeld, John *IRA:* 182

American Civil War
food preservation and *IRA:* 138
George Westinghouse and *IRB:* 185
government and *IRB:* 43
James J. Hill and *IRB:* 60
slavery and *IRB:* 196
tariffs and *IRA:* 195–196
telegraph and *IRB:* 11

American Declaration of Independence *IRA:* 9, 20, *IRB:* 84, *IRPS:* 195

American Federation of Labor *IRA:* 185 (ill.)
Congress of Industrial Organizations and *IRA:* 188
foundation of *IRA:* 185–186
government and *IRB:* 43–45
influence of *IRB:* 37
organization of *IRA:* 184, *IRB:* 41, *IRPS:* 100
purpose of *IRPS:* 112, 120

American Institute of Electrical Engineers *IRA:* 127

American Magazine IRB: 124, 127

American Railway Union *IRA:* 180–181

American Revolution *IRA:* 9, 30, 48, 209

American system *IRA:* 145 (ill.). *See also* Factory system; Manufacturing
development of *IRA:* 144–147, *IRB:* 16
impact of *IRB:* 27
productivity and *IRB:* 22–23
standardization and *IRA:* 223

American Telegraph Company *IRB:* 111

American Telephone and Telegraph (AT&T) *IRA:* 168, *IRB:* 99

American Union Telegraph *IRB:* 53

American Woolen Company *IRPS:* 164–166, 166–168, 168–169, 174–175

Amish *IRA:* 5 (ill.)

Anarchism
advocacy for *IRA:* 101, *IRB:* 85, *IRPS:* 150–151
definition of *IRA:* 84, 172
labor and *IRA:* 179–182
wealth and *IRPS:* 35, 38–40

Andrews, Samuel *IRA:* 166, *IRB:* 142

Animals *IRA:* 209–210, *IRB:* 200 (ill.). *See also* Horses; Livestock

Anti-Catholicism *IRB:* 109

Anti-Semitism *IRB:* 17, 25, 80, 109

Appert, Nicholas-François *IRA:* 137

Apprentices *IRA:* 10

Aristocracy. *See also* Feudalism; Medieval period
definition of *IRA:* 10
democracy and *IRA:* 6–7
Enlightenment and *IRA:* 21–22
industrialization and *IRA:* 4
Parliament and *IRA:* 86–87
progress and *IRA:* 6–7
religion and *IRA:* 13, 19–20

Arkwright, Richard *IRA:* 72 (ill.)
cotton mill of *IRA:* 109
spinning machine and *IRA:* 72, 110
textile factory of *IRA:* 77, 91, *IRPS:* 17

Art *IRA:* 13–14, *IRB:* 30–31, 102–103, 107–108, *IRPS:* 36

Ashley, Anthony Ashley Cooper, Lord *IRA:* 90–91, *IRPS:* 110

Asia *IRA:* 193, 214–215, 216–219. See also *specific countries*

Assembly lines *IRA:* 145 (ill.), 173 (ill.)
American system and *IRA:* 145, 146
automobiles and *IRB:* 22–23
definition of *IRA:* 144
development of *IRB:* 16
Henry Ford and *IRA:* 147, 148–151
impact of *IRB:* 27
standardization and *IRA:* 223

Associated Press *IRPS:* 84, 96

Automation *IRA:* 210, 216, *IRB:* 41

Automobiles *IRA:* 114 (ill.), 145 (ill.), 149 (ill.), 150 (ill.), *IRB:* 21 (ill.), 22 (ill.)
air pollution and *IRA:* 152–153, 212
assembly lines and *IRA:* 147, 148–151
competition and *IRA:* 218
internal combustion engine and *IRA:* 115–116
oil and *IRA:* 3, 151
production of *IRB:* 19–23, 24, 27
shock absorbers and *IRB:* 194
society and *IRA:* 116, 151–154, 158
tires and *IRA:* 132

B

Baekeland, Leo *IRA:* 132

Bakelite *IRA:* 132

Baker, Ray Stannard *IRB:* 123

Bakunin, Mikhail *IRA:* 101, *IRB:* 85

Balliol College *IRB:* 162–163, 163 (ill.)

Baltimore and Ohio Railroad *IRB:* 53

Bathhouses *IRPS:* 148, 153

The Battle with the Slum IRB: 118

Baxter, William *IRB:* 110

telegraph and *IRA:* 117–120

telephones and *IRA:* 120–122

Communism. *See also* Marxism; Socialism

definition of *IRA:* 84, 172, 210

development of *IRA:* 99–103, *IRB:* 80, 81–82, *IRPS:* 23–32

Great Depression and *IRA:* 203

impact of *IRPS:* 21–23, 24, 32

industrialization and *IRA:* 218–219

labor and *IRPS:* 62

Lincoln Steffens and *IRB:* 124, 125

wealth and *IRPS:* 34–35, 39–40

Communist League *IRB:* 81, *IRPS:* 23

The Communist Manifesto *IRA:* 100–101, *IRB:* 81–82, 84, *IRPS:* **21–33**, 22 (ill.)

A Compendious History of the Cotton Manufacture IRA: 77, 93

Competition. *See also* Monopolies

automobiles and *IRA:* 218

capitalism and *IRB:* 144, 155–157, 161–162, 165–167, *IRPS:* 5, 37–38, 198

factory system and *IRPS:* 56, 59–61

government and *IRB:* 155–159, 166–167, *IRPS:* 177–178, 179–191, 198, 200–202

guild system and *IRA:* 28

J. P. Morgan and *IRB:* 103–104

labor and *IRA:* 93–96, *IRPS:* 46, 54–59, 61–62, 63–74

monopolies and *IRA:* 4, 156, 162, 163, 167, 168–169, 197–199, *IRB:* 104, 149, 155–158

muckrakers and *IRA:* 162, 163, *IRB:* 115–116, 126–127

oil and *IRA:* 163, 166–167, 198–199, *IRB:* 116

railroads and *IRA:* 167, 197–198, *IRB:* 50–51, 55–56, 58–59, 60–67, 96–97, 157, *IRPS:* 88–89, 179–189

robber barons and *IRA:* 4

Sherman Antitrust Act and *IRB:* 144–145

socialism and *IRB:* 144, 153–154

steamboats and *IRB:* 34

steel and *IRA:* 168–169

technology and *IRPS:* 46

textiles and *IRA:* 93–96, *IRPS:* 56, 59–61

Computers *IRA:* 2, 210, 215–216, *IRB:* 106, *IRPS:* 73–74. *See also* Internet

The Condition of the Working Class in England IRPS: 110

Congress of Industrial Organizations *IRA:* 186, 188–189, *IRB:* 41, 42, *IRPS:* 120

Construction *IRA:* 163, *IRB:* 13

Continuous inventions *IRA:* 112, 215

Cooke, Jay *IRB:* 61

Cooke, William *IRPS:* 78

Cooperatives

anarchism and *IRA:* 101

factory system and *IRB:* 130, 134–136

Hull House and *IRPS:* 149, 152–154

labor unions and *IRB:* 42–43

Copernicus, Nicolaus *IRA:* 13

Corporations. *See also* Stockholders

definition of *IRA:* 144

factory system and *IRPS:* 23

muckrakers and *IRA:* 162–163

organization of *IRA:* 4–5

society and *IRPS:* 198

stockholders and *IRB:* 100

Cosmopolitan IRA: 162

Cottage industries. *See also* Craftsmanship

agriculture and *IRA:* 134

craftsmanship and *IRA:* 3–4, 211–212

definition of *IRA:* 10, 64, 210

factory system and *IRB:* 9, *IRPS:* 23, 102

guild system and *IRA:* 28–29

labor and *IRA:* 66–67

society and *IRPS:* 36–37

textiles and *IRA:* 28–29, 63, 66–67, 78, *IRB:* 9, *IRPS:* 54, 102

women and *IRA:* 68

Cotton

slavery and *IRA:* 64, 74

textiles and *IRA:* 66, 67, 109, *IRPS:* 60

Cotton gin *IRA:* 65 (ill.), *IRB:* 200 (ill.), 202 (ill.)

definition of *IRA:* 64

impact of *IRB:* 196

invention of *IRA:* 73–74, *IRB:* 199–202

slavery and *IRA:* 64, *IRB:* 196

Craftsmanship *IRA:* 2, 3–4, 211–212. *See also* Cottage industries

Craig, James *IRB:* 179

Crane, W. Murray *IRB:* 154

Crimean War *IRB:* 4

Crompton, Samuel *IRA:* 72–73

Culver, Helen *IRPS:* 152

The Curse of the Factory System IRA: 86

Cylinders

definition of *IRA:* 36, 75

operation of *IRA:* 37, 42, 43, 45–47, 113, *IRB:* 18, 19, *IRPS:* 47–48

steam locomotives and *IRA:* 53–54

D

Dabney, Morgan and Company *IRB:* 96
Dailey, Thomas *IRPS:* 93
Daimler, Gottlieb *IRA:* 114 (ill.), 115, 148
Dale, David *IRB:* 132
Danger
   coal mines and *IRA:* 49–50, *IRB:* 76, 171, *IRPS:* 124, 125, 133–134
   factory system and *IRA:* 85, 89, 173, *IRB:* 70, 76, 83, 116, 120–121, 149, *IRPS:* 11–12, 99, 156–163, 164, 170–172, 177, 196, 197
Darlington Railway *IRB:* 171
Darwin, Erasmus *IRA:* 48
Das Kapital IRA: 100, *IRPS:* 32
Davidson, Thomas *IRPS:* 149
Davy, Humphrey *IRB:* 171
Dearborn Independent IRB: 25
Debs, Eugene *IRA:* 180, 181, *IRPS:* 193
Deere, John *IRA:* 135–136, *IRB:* 92, 93, *IRPS:* 87
Dehydration *IRA:* 138
Democracy
   Chartists and *IRA:* 97–98
   definition of *IRA:* 10
   Enlightenment and *IRA:* 21–22
   factory system and *IRA:* 6–7, 87–89
   French Revolution and *IRA:* 209
   Japan and *IRA:* 218
   Parliament and *IRA:* 86–89
   Renaissance and *IRA:* 20
Democratic Party
   business and *IRA:* 196, *IRPS:* 190, 195
   labor and *IRA:* 186, *IRB:* 37, 43–44
Denver and Rio Grande Railroad *IRB:* 55, 56
Depression. *See* Recessions
Descartes, René *IRA:* 15, 17 (ill.)

Detroit Automobile Company *IRA:* 148, *IRB:* 21
Detroit Edison Illuminating Company *IRB:* 20
Dexterity *IRPS:* 9–10, 18
Dickinson, H. W. *IRA:* 58, 60, *IRB:* 32–33
Discontinuous inventions *IRA:* 112, 215–216
Disease *IRB:* 72, 145–146, 170. *See also* Health
Distribution *IRA:* 125–127, *IRB:* 143, 184, 189, 193
Division of labor. *See* specialization
Dodge, General *IRPS:* 94–95
Dodge, Horace *IRA:* 148
Dodge, John *IRA:* 148
Douglas, Margaret *IRB:* 162
Drake, Edwin L. *IRA:* 112, 165
Drew, Daniel *IRB:* 50
Drexel, Morgan and Company *IRB:* 97
Drilling *IRB:* 143
Drinkwater, Peter *IRB:* 131
Drugs *IRA:* 222–223, *IRPS:* 145
Dry Dock Engine Company *IRB:* 18, 19
Duncan, Sherman and Company *IRB:* 96
Durand, Peter *IRA:* 137–138
Durant, Thomas *IRPS:* 89, 94, 95, 96
Dyes *IRA:* 131
Dynamite *IRA:* 131

E

Economy of scale *IRA:* 143–144. *See also* Efficiency
Edison, Thomas Alva
   electricity and *IRA:* 123–126, *IRB:* 187
   General Electric and *IRA:* 168
   Henry Ford and *IRB:* 20
   lighting and *IRB:* 142
   telegraph and *IRB:* 111

Edison Illuminating Company *IRA:* 148
Education. *See also* Literacy
   Adam Smith and *IRB:* 162–163, *IRPS:* 5
   children and *IRB:* 133, *IRPS:* 58, 68–69, 164, 170, 173–174, 197–198
   Eli Whitney and *IRB:* 197–199
   George Stephenson and *IRB:* 170–171
   George Westinghouse and *IRB:* 185
   Ida Tarbell and *IRB:* 125–126
   individualism and *IRB:* 17
   James Watt and *IRB:* 178
   Jane Addams and *IRPS:* 146
   John D. Rockefeller and *IRB:* 140
   J. P. Morgan and *IRB:* 96
   Karl Marx and *IRB:* 80–81, 86
   Lincoln Steffens and *IRB:* 122–123
   literacy and *IRB:* 38–39
   Luddites and *IRPS:* 64
   Mother Jones and *IRB:* 71
   muckrakers and *IRB:* 121
   Nikola Tesla and *IRB:* 188
   philanthropy and *IRB:* 145–146
   public *IRB:* 178
   Robert Owen and *IRB:* 130–131, 133–134
   Samuel F. B. Morse and *IRB:* 107
   service economy and *IRA:* 215
   standardization of *IRA:* 223
   Theodore Roosevelt and *IRB:* 150
   Upton Sinclair and *IRB:* 119
Edward I *IRA:* 48, 212
Efficiency *IRA:* 143–144, 152–153, *IRPS:* 10, 200. *See also* Productivity
Eisenhower, Dwight D. *IRA:* 193

Electricity
  basics of *IRB:* 182,
    190–191
  coal and *IRA:* 3, 52,
    111–112
  distribution of *IRA:*
    125–127, *IRB:* 184, 189,
    193
  engines and *IRA:* 1, 3,
    122–123, 127, *IRB:* 191,
    193
  factory system and *IRA:*
    127
  generation of *IRA:* 116,
    122, 125, *IRB:* 184, 187,
    189–190, 193
  lighting and *IRA:* 123,
    125, 127, *IRB:* 142,
    190–191
  networks and *IRA:* 154
  railroads and *IRB:* 191
  telegraph and *IRA:*
    116–117, 118–119, *IRB:*
    108–109, *IRPS:* 77, 79
  telephones and *IRA:* 120
  Tennessee Valley Authori-
    ty and *IRA:* 202–203
Empiricism *IRA:* 10, 15, 22,
  48. *See also* Science
Enclosure movement. *See
  also* Urbanization
  description of *IRA:* 23–24,
    25, 84
  factory system and *IRA:*
    76, 79, 96
  textiles and *IRA:* 66–67,
    76, 79
  wealth and *IRA:* 23–24
Energy *IRA:* 33–34, 35, 47,
  138
Engels, Friedrich *IRA:* 100,
  IRB: 81, 82, 84, *IRPS:* 32,
  110
Engines *IRA:* 1, 3, 47,
  122–123, 127, *IRB:* 191,
  193. *See also* Internal
  combustion engines;
  Steam engines
England. *See also* Parliament
  agriculture in *IRA:* 3,
    24–26
  capitalism in *IRA:* 29–30
  coal in *IRA:* 41–42, 112

colonialism of *IRA:* 27,
  29, 30, 76
democracy and *IRA:* 7
enclosure movement in
  IRA: 23–24, 25, 66–67,
  76, 79, 84, 96
Enlightenment and *IRA:*
  21
factory system and *IRA:*
  76–78, 83–86, 89–95
government and *IRA:* 20,
  86–89, 97–98
guilds in *IRA:* 27–29
industrial revolution in
  IRA: 1, 12, 22–23, 45,
  IRPS: 4–5, 11–12, 13–15
labor unions in *IRA:*
  103–104
mercantilism in *IRA:*
  26–27, 29–30, 76
railroads in *IRA:* 51–56
Renaissance and *IRA:* 40
Robert Fulton and *IRA:*
  59–60
socialism in *IRA:* 96–98
steam engines in *IRA:* 7
tariffs and *IRA:* 194
textiles and *IRA:* 67,
  76–78, 109–110, *IRPS:*
  65–66
urbanization of *IRA:* 83–84
Enlightenment *IRA:* 21–22
Environment
  air pollution *IRA:*
    152–153, 212–213
  coal and *IRA:* 48–49, 85,
    212, *IRPS:* 133–134
  factory system and *IRA:* 85
  industrialization and *IRA:*
    212–213, *IRPS:* 192
  refrigeration and *IRA:* 140
  water pollution *IRA:* 85,
    140
Erie Railroad Company *IRB:*
  50–51
Evans, Oliver *IRA:* 139
**"Eyewitness at the Trian-
  gle"** *IRPS:* **156–163**

F

Fabian society *IRPS:* 149

Factory Act of 1833 *IRA:*
  90–91, *IRPS:* 110
The Factory Girl's Last Day
  IRPS: 106
Factory system *IRA:* 80 (ill.),
  90 (ill.), 111 (ill.), *IRB:*
  83 (ill.), *IRPS:* 16 (ill.),
  165 (ill.). *See also* Manufacturing
  agriculture and *IRA:* 223,
    IRPS: 137–138
  capitalism and *IRA:* 76
  children and *IRA:* 4, 63,
    65, 77, 79–80, 89–91,
    175, 219, *IRB:* 9, 76–77,
    132, *IRPS:* 13, 18,
    54–55, 58, 68–69, 99,
    101–110, 114, 117, 119,
    120–122, 164–174, 177,
    203
  cigar making and *IRPS:*
    112–120
  coal and *IRA:* 49, 52
  competition and *IRPS:* 56,
    59–61
  cooperatives and *IRB:*
    130, 134–136
  cottage industries and
    IRPS: 23, 102
  dangers of *IRA:* 85, 173,
    IRB: 70, 76, 83, 116,
    120–121, 149, *IRPS:*
    11–12, 99, 156–163,
    164, 170–172, 177, 196,
    197
  democracy and *IRA:* 6–7,
    87–89
  electricity and *IRA:* 127
  enclosure movement and
    IRA: 76, 79, 96
  environment and *IRA:* 85
  government and *IRA:*
    6–7, 64, 89–91, 94–95,
    IRB: 134
  government regulation
    and *IRPS:* 101–102,
    106, 158, 162–163, 177
  hours and *IRA:* 4, 78, 85,
    86, 89, 91, 92, 150, 173,
    179, 182, *IRB:* 9, 23, 71,
    132–133, *IRPS:* 29, 55,
    99, 101–102, 103–110,
    117, 118, 177

housing and *IRB:* 71, 83, 133, *IRPS:* 112–122, 152–153

immigration and *IRPS:* 166

labor and *IRA:* 4, 78–81, 84–85, 85–86, *IRB:* 132–134, 203–204, *IRPS:* 1, 2, 13–19, 28–31, 54–59, 61–62, 63–74, 99–110, 112–122

labor unions and *IRPS:* 19, 100, 163

meat processing and *IRPS:* 135–145

muckrakers and *IRPS:* 135–145, 158

poverty and *IRA:* 96, 172–175, *IRB:* 69–70, 71

productivity and *IRA:* 76–78, 146, *IRPS:* 13–14, 19, 54–61, 63

property and *IRPS:* 23, 25–28

railroads and *IRA:* 52

refrigeration and *IRA:* 140

social reform and *IRA:* 91–93

society and *IRA:* 2, 3–6, 64–66, 78–81, 83–86, 171–175, *IRB:* 133–136

specialization in *IRPS:* 3–11

steel and *IRA:* 130

telegraph and *IRA:* 117, 121

textiles and *IRA:* 63–66, 76–78, 90–91, 192, 219, 222, *IRB:* 9, 76–77, 132, *IRPS:* 54–62, 63–74, 102, 156–163, 164–175, 203

urbanization and *IRA:* 5–6, 64, 83–84, 171, *IRPS:* 23

violence and *IRPS:* 104, 108, 109

wages and *IRA:* 4, 79, 80, 85, 89, 96, 150–151, 161–163, 172–173, 177, 180–181, 219, *IRB:* 9, 17, 23, 25, 26, 27, 39, 83, 120, 132, *IRPS:* 18,

19, 29–31, 64, 117, 118, 168, 169, 172, 177

wealth and *IRA:* 64, *IRPS:* 1, 2, 14, 15

women and *IRA:* 219, *IRPS:* 18, 29

wool and *IRA:* 95

work and *IRA:* 76, 78–79, 84–85, 85–86, 89–93, 96, 146, *IRB:* 27, *IRPS:* 13–19, 28–29, 103–109, 114–120, 136, 138–139, 140–141, 145, 168–174

Fair Labor Standards Act *IRPS:* 122

Faraday, Michael *IRA:* 85, 118, 120, 122, *IRB:* 108

Farming. *See* Agriculture

Federal Reserve Bank *IRB:* 102

Federal Trade Commission Act *IRA:* 197

Fermentation *IRA:* 139

Fertilizers *IRA:* 133, 134

Feudalism *IRA:* 4, 10, 13. *See also* Aristocracy; Medieval period

Fielden, John *IRA:* 86

Fillmore, Millard *IRPS:* 82–83

Finance. *See also* Business; Capital
agriculture and *IRB:* 93, 101–102
government and *IRA:* 21, 22, 155, *IRB:* 95, 101–102, 109–110
interest and *IRA:* 19, 220–221
J. P. Morgan and *IRA:* 167–169, *IRB:* 14, 64–66, 95, 96–97, 99–102, 103–104, 157, 191
networks and *IRA:* 154–155
oil and *IRA:* 165, 166
panic of 1907 and *IRB:* 193
radio and *IRB:* 191
railroads and *IRA:* 154–155, 159–160, 168, *IRB:* 47–48, 49–53, 64–66, 96–97, 157

Reformation and *IRA:* 19

regulation of *IRPS:* 200, 202

steamboats and *IRA:* 58

steam engines and *IRA:* 44

steel and *IRA:* 168–169, *IRB:* 14, 66, 101, 104

telegraph and *IRA:* 120, *IRB:* 106, 107, 109–110, *IRPS:* 76, 77, 78, 82–83, 84

Fisk, Jim *IRB:* 47, 50

Fitch, John *IRA:* 57, *IRB:* 32

Flagler, Henry M. *IRB:* 142

Flying shuttle *IRA:* 75

Food *IRPS:* 141 (ill.). *See also* Agriculture
preservation of *IRA:* 134, 136–140
price of *IRA:* 95
processing of *IRB:* 116, 120, 121, 122, 149, *IRPS:* 135–145
railroads and *IRA:* 121
regulation of *IRA:* 163, *IRPS:* 136–137, 144–145
standardization and *IRA:* 223
urbanization and *IRA:* 83–84

Food and Drug Act of 1906 *IRA:* 163, *IRB:* 120, 122, *IRPS:* 144–145

Ford, Clara (Bryant) *IRB:* 19

Ford, Edsel *IRB:* 19, 27

Ford, Henry *IRB:* **16** (ill.), **16–27,** 21 (ill.)
assembly line developed by *IRA:* 147, *IRB:* 16
automobiles and *IRA:* 148–151, *IRB:* 19–23, 27
early life of *IRA:* 147–148, *IRB:* 17–19, 96
labor and *IRA:* 150–151, 177, *IRB:* 17, 23–24, 25–27
muckrakers and *IRB:* 127
reputation of *IRB:* 24–25
social innovation by *IRA:* 150–151, *IRB:* 23–24
tractors and *IRA:* 136

Ford, Henry, II *IRB:* 27

Ford, John *IRA:* 147

Ford, William *IRB:* 17

Ford Motor Company *IRA:* 147, 148–151, 173 (ill.), *IRB:* 21–24, 27

Forgery *IRB:* 2–3

Foster, Jonathan *IRB:* 173

Frame Breaking Act *IRA:* 94–95, *IRPS:* 73

France *IRA:* 21, 26–27, 29, 58–59. *See also* French Revolution

Frankenstein, Richard T. *IRB:* 26 (ill.)

Franklin, Benjamin *IRA:* 48, 122, *IRB:* 30–31

Fraternal orders *IRA:* 190–191. *See also* Labor unions

Freedom of speech *IRA:* 98, 100, 103–104, *IRB:* 81

Freezing *IRA:* 138

French and Indian War *IRA:* 23, 30

French Revolution
description of *IRA:* 9, 209
England and *IRB:* 202
Luddites and *IRA:* 95, *IRPS:* 66
Lunar Society and *IRA:* 48
Reform Bill of 1832 and *IRA:* 88
socialism and *IRA:* 96, 97

Frick, Henry Clay *IRA:* 162, 163, *IRB:* 12, 13

Fulton, Elizabeth *IRB:* 31

Fulton, Mary (Smith) *IRB:* 30, 31

Fulton, Robert *IRA:* 57–60, 59 (ill.), *IRB:* 29 (ill.), **29–35**

Fulton, Robert (inventor's father) *IRB:* 30

G

Gagging Acts *IRA:* 98, 103–104

Galileo Galilei *IRA:* 13

Gamble, Mr. *IRPS:* 95

Gary, Elbert H. *IRB:* 127

Gas *IRA:* 121. *See also* Gasoline; Oil

Gaskell, Philip *IRA:* 85–86

Gasoline *IRA:* 136, 151, *IRB:* 19. *See also* Gas; Oil

Gaulard, Lucient *IRB:* 193

General Education Board *IRB:* 146

General Electric Company *IRA:* 168, 215, *IRB:* 99

General Motors Company *IRB:* 24, 26

George Peabody and Company *IRB:* 96

German Workers' Party *IRB:* 81

Germany *IRA:* 17–19, 51, 205, *IRB:* 3–4, 25

Germinal *IRPS:* **123–134**

Gibbs, John *IRB:* 193

Gilbert, William *IRA:* 122

Global warming *IRA:* 212–213

God *IRA:* 13, 14, 19–20. *See also* Religion

Gold *IRA:* 27, *IRB:* 52, 101–102, 193

Gompers, Samuel *IRA:* 185 (ill.), *IRB:* 37 (ill.), **37–45** *IRPS:* 113 (ill.)
cigar making and *IRA:* 184, *IRB:* 38–39, *IRPS:* **112–120**
early life of *IRB:* 38–39
labor unions and *IRA:* 184–186, *IRB:* 37–38, 39–45, *IRPS:* 100, 112, 120, 122
politics and *IRB:* 43–45

Gompers, Sarah (Rood) *IRB:* 38

Gompers, Solomon *IRB:* 38

Goodyear, Charles *IRA:* 132

Gorrie, John *IRA:* 139

The Gospel of Wealth *IRA:* 164

Gould, Edith (Kingdon) *IRB:* 56–57

Gould, George Jay *IRB:* 47, 53–57

Gould, Helen Day (Miller) *IRB:* 49

Gould, Jason *IRB:* 48

Gould, Jay *IRB:* 47 (ill.), **47–54**, 55

Government. *See also* Government regulation; Politics; *specific governmental bodies; specific political parties*
business and *IRA:* 188, 196, *IRB:* 158, *IRPS:* 195
coal and *IRB:* 154–155
competition and *IRB:* 155–159, 166–167
corruption in *IRPS:* 113, 115
Enlightenment and *IRA:* 21–22
factory system and *IRA:* 6–7, 64, 94–95, *IRB:* 134
finance and *IRA:* 21, 22, 155, *IRB:* 95, 101–102, 109–110, *IRPS:* 76, 77, 78, 82–83
God and *IRA:* 19–20
labor and *IRB:* 13, 42, 43–45, 74–76, *IRPS:* 62, 166, 167, 203
labor suppressed by *IRA:* 103–104, 162, 178–179, 179–183, 187, 188, 189–190
labor unions and *IRA:* 103–104, 178–179, 181, 186, 188–189, 203–204, 205
Marxism and *IRB:* 81–82, 84–85
Medieval period and *IRA:* 87
muckrakers and *IRB:* 114, 116, 119, 120, 122, 123–125
poverty and *IRA:* 194, 199–205
railroads and *IRA:* 155, *IRB:* 60–61, 61–62
reform of *IRA:* 86–89, 97–98, *IRPS:* 14, 200
rifles and *IRB:* 202–203
socialism and *IRA:* 96–101, 176
social work and *IRPS:* 153, 154

telegraph and *IRB:* 106, 107, 109–110, *IRPS:* 76, 77, 78, 82–83

wealth and *IRA:* 19–20, 86–89, 194

Government regulation. See also *specific governmental bodies; specific laws*
children and *IRPS:* 106, 122, 164, 177
coal and *IRB:* 154–155
environment and *IRA:* 212–213
factory system and *IRA:* 89–91, *IRPS:* 101–102, 106, 158, 162–163, 177
food processing and *IRB:* 120, *IRPS:* 136–137, 144–145
growth of *IRA:* 192–193
hours and *IRPS:* 165, 167, 177, 196–197
labor and *IRA:* 103–104, 179, 188–189, 196, 202–205
labor unions and *IRB:* 42, 43–45, 154–155
laissez-faire and *IRA:* 10, 29–30, 192
monopolies and *IRA:* 4, 163, 167, 197–199, *IRB:* 58, 59, 64–66, 139, 143–145, 148–149, 155–159, 166–167, *IRPS:* 97, 137, 177–178, 179–191, 192, 194, 200–202
muckrakers and *IRA:* 162–163
oil and *IRB:* 139, 157
patents and *IRPS:* 199
poverty and *IRA:* 199–205
property and *IRA:* 20
railroads and *IRA:* 197–198, *IRB:* 58, 59, 64–66, 157
social reform and *IRB:* 119, 161–162, *IRPS:* 192–203
steel and *IRB:* 66
strikes and *IRA:* 188–189, 203–204, 205

tariffs and *IRA:* 109, 172, 193–196
taxes and *IRA:* 196–197, *IRPS:* 35, 43, 199
textiles and *IRA:* 109–110
Theodore Roosevelt and *IRPS:* 158, 177–178, 182, 190
wages and *IRPS:* 106, 122, 177, 196–197

Grace, William *IRPS:* 115
Grand Central Station *IRB:* 49 (ill.)
Grand National Consolidated Trade Union *IRA:* 92, *IRB:* 136–137
Gray, Elisha *IRA:* 120
Great Chicago Fire of 1871 *IRB:* 72 (ill.), 72–73, 93
Great Depression *IRA:* 199–205, 201 (ill.), *IRB:* 25, 125. See also Recessions
Great Northern Railroad building of *IRPS:* 87
Louis Hill and *IRB:* 67
monopolies and *IRA:* 197–198, *IRB:* 65, 66, 157, *IRPS:* 179, 183–186
Greece *IRA:* 122
Greene, Catherine *IRA:* 73, *IRB:* 196, 199
Grey, Charles Grey, Second Earl *IRA:* 88
Grosscup, Peter S. *IRA:* 181
Guest, Richard *IRA:* 77, 93
Guilds *IRA:* 10, 27–29, 103
Guizot, François *IRPS:* 24
Gutenberg, Johannes *IRA:* 16–17

H

Hackworth, Timothy *IRB:* 173
Halls of Science *IRB:* 135
Hargreaves, James *IRA:* 69–72
Harkness, S. V. *IRB:* 142
Harlan, John Marshall *IRPS:* 182–189, 184 (ill.)

Harriman, Edward H. *IRB:* 55–56, 65–66, 66–67
Harris, Mary. See Mary Harris Jones
Harrison, Benjamin *IRB:* 151
Hart, Mr. *IRPS:* 94
Hautefeuille, Jean de *IRA:* 44
Haymarket Square Riot *IRA:* 179–182
Health *IRPS:* 199. See also Danger; Disease
Heat *IRB:* 180
Heating *IRA:* 138
Hedley, William *IRA:* 55, *IRB:* 173
Hegel, Georg Wilhelm Friedrich *IRB:* 80
Henry, Joseph *IRA:* 118, *IRB:* 110
Henry Ford Company *IRA:* 148. See also Ford Motor Company
Henry the Navigator, Prince *IRA:* 14
Hero *IRA:* 38
Hewitt and Tuttle *IRB:* 140, 141–142
Hill, James J. *IRB:* 58 (ill.)
early life of *IRB:* 59–60
monopolies and *IRB:* 64–67, 157, *IRPS:* 179, 180, 183–186, 189
railroads and *IRB:* 58–59, 60–67, 157, *IRPS:* 87, 179, 180, 183–186, 189
Hill, Louis *IRB:* 67
History of the Erie Canal IRB: 31
The History of the Standard Oil Company IRB: 127, 156
Hitler, Adolf *IRB:* 17, 25
Holmes, Oliver Wendell *IRPS:* 181
Holocaust *IRB:* 25
Homestead Strike *IRA:* 161–163, *IRB:* 12, 13
Homfray, Samuel *IRA:* 54
Hoover, Herbert *IRA:* 203
Horsepower *IRPS:* 53
Horses *IRA:* 5 (ill.)

agriculture and *IRA:* 135, 136, *IRB:* 89

coal and *IRA:* 41, *IRPS:* 47, 125

machines and *IRA:* 209–210

productivity and *IRPS:* 50–51

railroads and *IRA:* 51, 53

spinning machines and *IRA:* 72

transportation and *IRA:* 158

Horsfall, William *IRA:* 94–95

Hours

Chartists and *IRPS:* 13

children and *IRA:* 4, 85, 86, 89, 91, *IRPS:* 54–55, 99, 104, 106, 107–109, 110

factory system and *IRA:* 4, 78, 85, 86, 89, 91, 92, 150, 173, 179, 182, *IRB:* 9, 23, 71, 132–133, *IRPS:* 29, 55, 99, 101–102, 103–110, 117, 118, 177

Henry Ford and *IRB:* 23

labor unions and *IRA:* 179–182, 187

productivity and *IRPS:* 104

regulation of *IRPS:* 165, 167, 177, 196–197

Robert Owen and *IRB:* 132–133

strikes and *IRA:* 179, 182, 187

Housing *IRA:* 200 (ill.), *IRPS:* 116 (ill.)

factory system and *IRA:* 78, 80, *IRB:* 71, 83, 133, *IRPS:* 112–122, 152–153

muckrakers and *IRB:* 114–115, 116, 117–119

society and *IRA:* 174–175, *IRPS:* 152–153

strikes and *IRA:* 180–181

How the Other Half Lives IRA: 162, *IRB:* 118

Hull, Charles J. *IRPS:* 151, 152

Hull House *IRA:* 191–192, *IRPS:* 146–154, 150 (ill.)

Hulls, Jonathan *IRA:* 56

Hume, David *IRA:* 21, 22, 29

Huygens, Christian *IRA:* 44, 114

Hyatt, John Wesley *IRA:* 132

I

Immigration

business owners and *IRB:* 39

factory system and *IRPS:* 166

labor and *IRA:* 176–177

muckrakers and *IRB:* 115, 118–119

politics and *IRB:* 109

railroads and *IRB:* 60–61, 63–64, *IRPS:* 87, 89, 93

social work and *IRPS:* 146–154

society and *IRA:* 199, *IRPS:* 199

India *IRA:* 68

Individualism *IRA:* 176, *IRB:* 17, 26, *IRPS:* 39–40

Indonesia *IRA:* 219

Industrial Revolution

beginning of *IRA:* 9–12

first stage of *IRA:* 1, 112

overview of *IRA:* 1–2, 209–212

second stage of *IRA:* 1, 107–108, 112, 205

third stage of *IRA:* 2, 193, 215–216

Industrial Workers of the World *IRB:* 45, *IRPS:* 166–168

An Inquiry Into the Natures and Causes of the Wealth of Nations

government regulation and *IRA:* 29, 192, *IRB:* 161, 165–167

Karl Marx and *IRPS:* 32

mercantilism and *IRA:* 30, *IRB:* 164–165

specialization and *IRPS:* **3–11**

Institute for the Formation of Character *IRA:* 92, *IRB:* 133

Interchangeable parts. *See also* Standardization

assembly lines and *IRA:* 145–146, 146–147

definition of *IRA:* 144

development of *IRB:* 16

humans as *IRA:* 4, 80–81, 223

rifles and *IRB:* 197, 203–204

Interest *IRA:* 19, 220–221. *See also* Finance

Internal combustion engines

automobiles and *IRB:* 19–21

development of *IRA:* 114–116, 148, *IRB:* 18, 142

oil and *IRA:* 1, 113

operation of *IRA:* 3, 113–114, *IRB:* 19

International and Great Northern Railroad *IRB:* 55

International Harvester *IRA:* 168, *IRB:* 99

International Ladies Garment Workers Union *IRPS:* 163

International trade *IRA:* 217, 218. *See also* Colonialism; Mercantilism

International Workingman's Association *IRB:* 84–85

Internet. *See also* Computers

communications and *IRA:* 117

development of *IRPS:* 83–84

industrial revolution and *IRA:* 2

Luddites and *IRPS:* 73–74

networks and *IRA:* 154

standardization and *IRA:* 155

telegraph and *IRB:* 106

Interstate Commerce Commission *IRPS:* 199, 202
Inventions *IRA:* 112, 215–216. See also *specific inventions*
Investment. *See* Finance
Iran *IRA:* 220, 221 (ill.)
Iraq *IRA:* 220
Iron. *See also* Steel
coal and *IRA:* 49, 52
properties of *IRB:* 4
railroads and *IRA:* 52–53, 157, 161
steam engines and *IRA:* 45
steel and *IRA:* 127–130
Iron Molders International Union *IRB:* 71, 72
Islam *IRA:* 220–221

J

J. P. Morgan and Company *IRB:* 97
Jackson, Andrew *IRA:* 195
Japan *IRA:* 205, 217–218
Jefferson, Thomas *IRA:* 20, 48, 108, *IRB:* 33–34, *IRPS:* 195
Jet engine *IRA:* 57
Joffroy d'Abbans, Marquis de *IRA:* 56
John (king of England) *IRA:* 20
Johnson, Caleb *IRB:* 30
Johnson, Cave *IRPS:* 83
Johnson, Lyndon *IRB:* 122
Jolliet, Louis *IRA:* 52
Jones, Ernest *IRB:* 131
Jones, George *IRA:* 184, *IRB:* 71–72
Jones, Mary Harris (Mother Jones) *IRA:* 182 (ill.), 183–184, *IRB:* 69 (ill.), **69–78**
Journalism *IRB:* 81, 82, 115 (ill.), 121. *See also* Muckrakers; Newspapers
Joyce, Patrick *IRPS:* 93
The Jungle IRA: 163, *IRB:* 116, 120–121, 156, *IRPS:* **135–145**

K

Kay, John *IRA:* 72, 75
Kelly, William *IRA:* 129–130, *IRB:* 6
Kennedy, Michael *IRPS:* 93
Keyser, Mary *IRPS:* 152
Killeen, Edward *IRPS:* 93
King Coal IRB: 121
Kittson, Norman *IRB:* 60
Knights of Labor *IRA:* 179–182, 191, *IRB:* 73
Know-Nothing Party *IRB:* 109
Knox, John *IRB:* 178
Koerner, Thomas *IRPS:* 150
Kuwait *IRA:* 220

L

Labor *IRA:* 80 (ill.), 133 (ill.), 183 (ill.), 187 (ill.), 189 (ill.), *IRB:* 42 (ill.), 83 (ill.), 192 (ill.), *IRPS:* 55 (ill.), 91 (ill.), 128 (ill.). *See also* Labor unions; Work
anarchism and *IRA:* 179–182
benefits for *IRA:* 173–174, 188, 189–190, 191, *IRB:* 40–41, *IRPS:* 35
cigar making and *IRPS:* 112–120
coal and *IRB:* 73–76, 154–155, *IRPS:* 123–134
communism and *IRPS:* 23, 28–31, 62
competition and *IRA:* 93–96, *IRPS:* 46, 54–59, 61–62, 63–74
conditions for *IRB:* 69–70
cottage industries and *IRA:* 66–67
factory system and *IRA:* 4, 78–81, 84–85, 85–86, *IRB:* 132–134, 203–204, *IRPS:* 1, 2, 13–19, 28–31, 54–59, 61–62, 63–74, 99–100, 112–122
government and *IRPS:* 62, 166, 167, 203
government regulates *IRA:* 103–104, 179, 188–189, 196, 202–205
government suppresses *IRA:* 103–104, 162, 178–179, 179–183, 187, 188, 189–190
guild system and *IRA:* 10, 27–29, 103
Henry Ford and *IRB:* 17, 23–24, 25–27
immigration and *IRA:* 176–177
as interchangeable parts *IRA:* 4, 80–81, 223
lockouts of *IRA:* 92
Luddites and *IRA:* 93–96
machines and *IRPS:* 54–59, 61–62, 63–74
management of *IRA:* 152–153
Marxism and *IRB:* 79–80, 81–82, 83–85
meat processing and *IRPS:* 136, 138–139, 140–141, 145
productivity and *IRPS:* 54–61, 63
railroads and *IRB:* 64
Revolution of 1848 and *IRB:* 81–82
rights of *IRA:* 6–7, *IRB:* 41–42, *IRPS:* 5, 196–198
slavery and *IRB:* 120
socialism and *IRA:* 96–97, 176, 179–182, 184, 186, 190, *IRB:* 23, 37, 39–40, 43, 44, 45, 130, 132–136, *IRPS:* 62
specialization and *IRPS:* 3–11
steam engines and *IRPS:* 18
steel and *IRB:* 12, 13
textiles and *IRA:* 93–96, *IRPS:* 54–59, 61–62, 63–74, 101–110, 164–175
unemployment and *IRPS:* 54–59, 61–62, 66, 68
voluntary associations of *IRA:* 190–191

Labor unions. *See also* Labor; Strikes

American Federation of Labor *IRA:* 184, 185 (ill.), 185–186, 188, *IRB:* 37, 41, 43–45, *IRPS:* 100, 112, 120

American Railway Union *IRA:* 180–181

business opposition to *IRA:* 161–162, 176

Cigarmakers' Union *IRB:* 38, 40–41

cigar making and *IRPS:* 112, 120

coal and *IRA:* 182–184, 186–188, 189–190

Congress of Industrial Organizations *IRA:* 186, 188–189, *IRB:* 41, 42, *IRPS:* 120

definition of *IRA:* 172, 210

early examples of *IRA:* 92–93, 102–104

factory system and *IRPS:* 19, 100, 163

government and *IRA:* 103–104, 178–179, 181, 186, 188–189, 203–204, 205, *IRB:* 42, 43–45, 154–155

Grand National Consolidated Trade Union *IRA:* 92, *IRB:* 136–137

growth of *IRA:* 177–178, *IRB:* 41

Haymarket Square Riot and *IRA:* 179–182

Homestead Strike and *IRA:* 161–163, *IRB:* 12, 13

hours and *IRA:* 179–182, 187

Industrial Workers of the World *IRB:* 45, *IRPS:* 166–168

influence of *IRB:* 37–38

International Ladies Garment Workers Union *IRPS:* 163

Iron Molders International Union *IRB:* 71, 72

Knights of Labor *IRA:* 179–182, 191, *IRB:* 73

Luddites and *IRA:* 95

as monopolies *IRA:* 181

Pullman strike and *IRA:* 180–181

purpose of *IRA:* 175–176, 186, *IRB:* 38, 40–41, 41–43, *IRPS:* 122

railroads and *IRA:* 180–181

Robert Owen and *IRB:* 136–137

United Automobile Workers Union *IRB:* 17, 25–27

United Mine Workers Union *IRA:* 184, 186–188, 189–190, *IRB:* 73, 74, 154–155

violence and *IRA:* 162–163, 179–183

voluntary associations *IRA:* 190–191

wages and *IRA:* 95, 161–163, 178, 180–181, *IRPS:* 100, 166–168, 174–175

Lacy, Charles *IRA:* 94, *IRPS:* 66–67

La Follette, Robert, Jr. *IRPS:* 203

La Follette, Robert, Sr. *IRPS:* 203

Laissez-faire *IRA:* 10, 29–30, 192, *IRB:* 152–153, 166. *See also* Government regulation

Land *IRA:* 23–24, *IRB:* 60, *IRPS:* 87

"Last Tie" *IRPS:* **85–97**

Latin America *IRA:* 222–253

Laurrell, Ferdinand *IRB:* 40

Lawrence Textile Strike of 1912 *IRPS:* 164–166, 166–168, 174–175, 203

Laws. *See* Government regulation

"Leeds Cloth Merchants Proclamation in Support of Machinery" *IRPS:* **54–62**

Leeds Intelligencer IRPS: 56

Leeds Mercury IRPS: 56

Lenin, Vladimir *IRB:* 124

Lenoir, Jean-Joseph-Étienne *IRA:* 114

Leonardo da Vinci *IRA:* 13

Leupp, C. M. *IRB:* 48

Lewis, John L. *IRA:* 186–188, 189–190, *IRB:* 74

Libraries *IRB:* 14, *IRPS:* 42, 148, 153

The Life of Abraham Lincoln IRB: 126

Lighting
coal mines and *IRB:* 171
electricity and *IRA:* 123, 125, 127, *IRB:* 182, 190–191
gas and *IRA:* 121
General Electric and *IRA:* 168
oil and *IRB:* 142
standardization and *IRA:* 155

Lincoln, Abraham *IRB:* 126, *IRPS:* 195

Literacy *IRA:* 16–17, *IRB:* 38–39, *IRPS:* 64, 66, 197–198. *See also* Education

Little Sisters of the Poor *IRPS:* 151

Liverpool and Manchester Railway *IRB:* 174–175

Livestock *IRPS:* 135–145. *See also* Food

Livingston, Robert *IRA:* 58, 60, *IRB:* 32, 34

Locke, John *IRA:* 20, 21

Lockouts *IRA:* 92

Locomotion IRB: 174

Lombe, Sir Thomas *IRPS:* 17

London Workingman's Association *IRA:* 97

Looms *IRA:* 64, 68–69, 75–76, *IRPS:* 170 (ill.)

Louisiana Purchase *IRA:* 108, *IRB:* 33

Louis Phillipe (king of France) *IRA:* 100

Louis XVI *IRA:* 97

Lovett, William *IRA:* 97

Ludd, Ned *IRA:* 93–94, *IRPS:* 61–62, 64, 65
Luddites *IRA:* 93–96, 175, *IRPS:* 46, **61–62, 63–74**
Ludlow Massacre *IRB:* 75 (ill.)
Lunar Society *IRA:* 48, *IRB:* 182, *IRPS:* 12
Luther, Martin *IRA:* 18–19

M

MacArthur, Douglas *IRA:* 203
Machiavelli, Niccolò *IRA:* 13–14, 14 (ill.)
Machines. See also *specific machines*
  energy and *IRA:* 33–34, 47
  engines compared with *IRA:* 47
  humans and *IRA:* 209–212
  interchangeable parts and *IRA:* 146
  labor and *IRPS:* 54–59, 61–62, 63–74
  specialization and *IRPS:* 10–11
  textiles and *IRA:* 1, 63–66, *IRPS:* 54–62
Machine tools *IRB:* 203, *IRPS:* 10–11
Magna Carta *IRA:* 6, 20
Mail *IRPS:* 75, 199
Malaysia *IRA:* 219
Malthus, Thomas *IRA:* 83–84, 85 (ill.)
Management *IRA:* 147, 152–153. See also Business
Manchester Literary and Philosophical Society *IRA:* 91–92, *IRB:* 131–132
Manhattan Elevated Railroad *IRB:* 54
Mannucci, Aldo *IRA:* 17
Manufacturing *IRA:* 145 (ill.). See also Factory system

American system of *IRA:* 144–147, 223, *IRB:* 16, 22–23, 27
communications and *IRB:* 106–107, 112
competition and *IRPS:* 37–38
Henry Ford and *IRA:* 147, 148–151
plows and *IRA:* 135–136
railroads and *IRB:* 61
rifles and *IRB:* 197, 202–204
society and *IRA:* 213–215, *IRPS:* 37
specialization and *IRPS:* 3–11
technology and *IRA:* 3
The Manufacturing Population of England IRA: 85–86
Marconi, Guglielmo *IRB:* 190
Marquette, Père *IRA:* 52
Marshall, John *IRPS:* 110
Marx, Heinrich *IRB:* 80
Marx, Henriette Presburg *IRB:* 80
Marx, Jenny (von Westphalen) *IRB:* 80, 86
Marx, Karl *IRA:* 99 (ill.), *IRB:* **79–87**, 79 (ill.), *IRPS:* **21–33,** 25 (ill.), 31 (ill.)
  character of *IRB:* 85–86, *IRPS:* 32–33
  early life of *IRB:* 80–81
  influence of *IRPS:* 21–23, 32
  Marxism and *IRA:* 99–103, *IRB:* 79–80, 81–85, 136, *IRPS:* 2, 23–32
  Samuel Gompers and *IRB:* 39
Marxism *IRA:* 99–103, *IRB:* 79–80, 81–85, *IRPS:* 2, 21–32. See also Communism; Socialism
Mass production *IRA:* 144. See also Factory system; Manufacturing
McBride, John *IRA:* 186
McClure, S. S. *IRB:* 123

McClure's magazine *IRA:* 163, 167, *IRB:* 123–124, 126–127, 156
McCormick, Cyrus *IRA:* 136 (ill.), *IRB:* 88 (ill.), **88–93**
  company of *IRA:* 168, 179, *IRB:* 93, 99
  early life of *IRB:* 88–90
  reapers and *IRA:* 134–135, *IRB:* 88, 90–93, 99, *IRPS:* 87
McCormick, Leander *IRB:* 91–92, 93
McCormick, Mary Ann Hall *IRB:* 89
McCormick, Robert *IRB:* 88–90
McCormick, William *IRB:* 91–92
McCormick Harvester *IRA:* 168, 179, *IRB:* 93, 99
McGuffey, William *IRB:* 17
McKinley, William *IRB:* 148, 151, 152, *IRPS:* 192
McNamara, Frederick *IRPS:* 93
Meat *IRPS:* 135–145. See also Food
Mechanical power *IRA:* 3. See also Machines
Medieval period. See also Aristocracy; Feudalism
  alchemy in *IRA:* 130
  definition of *IRA:* 10
  government in *IRA:* 87
  religion during *IRA:* 13, 14
  Renaissance and *IRA:* 12
  wealth and *IRA:* 22
Mercantilism. See also Colonialism
  colonialism and *IRA:* 20–21, 27, 29, 30, 76, *IRB:* 165
  description of *IRA:* 10, 26–27, *IRB:* 164–165
  in England *IRA:* 26–27, 76
Merchants *IRA:* 27–29, 67
Metallurgy *IRA:* 127–130, *IRB:* 2. See also Bessemer process; Steel

Metro-Goldwyn-Mayer *IRB:* 122

The Metropolis IRB: 121

Metropolitan Museum of Art *IRB:* 103, 103 (ill.)

Metternich, Klemens von *IRPS:* 24

Mexican-American War *IRA:* 108

Mexico *IRB:* 124

Michelangelo *IRA:* 13

Michigan Car Works *IRB:* 18

Microchips *IRA:* 210, 216. *See also* Computers

Middle Ages. *See* Medieval period

Middle East *IRA:* 151, 220–221

Middleton Railway *IRA:* 52

Military *IRB:* 5 (ill.)
  industrialization and *IRA:* 205, *IRB:* 17
  Internet and *IRPS:* 83–84
  rifles and *IRB:* 197, 202–204
  steel and *IRB:* 4–6
  telegraph and *IRB:* 11

Miller, Patrick *IRA:* 56

Miller, Phineas *IRB:* 198–199, 200, 201

Mills *IRA:* 109–111, *IRPS:* 49–50. *See also* Factory system; Textiles

Mills, Edgar *IRPS:* 95

Milwaukee Journal IRPS: 156

***The Miner's Friend** IRPS:* **47–52**

Mississippi River Steamboat Company *IRB:* 59–60

Missouri Pacific Railroad *IRB:* 52–53, 55–56

Model A *IRB:* 22, 24

Model T *IRA:* 149 (ill.), 150 (ill.), *IRB:* 22 (ill.)
  cost of *IRA:* 149, *IRB:* 16, 18, 23
  production of *IRA:* 147, 149–150, *IRB:* 22–23, 24

Money *IRPS:* 114. *See also* Finance

The Moneychangers IRB: 121

Monopolies. *See also* Competition

competition and *IRA:* 4, 156, 162, 163, 167, 168–169, 197–199, *IRB:* 104, 149, 155–158

definition of *IRA:* 144, 172, *IRB:* 144–145

government regulation and *IRA:* 4, 163, 167, 197–199, *IRB:* 58, 59, 64–66, 139, 143–145, 148–149, 155–159, 166–167, *IRPS:* 97, 137, 177–178, 179–191, 192, 194, 200–202

J. P. Morgan and *IRA:* 168–169

labor unions as *IRA:* 181

muckrakers and *IRA:* 162, 163, *IRB:* 126–127, 156

oil and *IRA:* 163, 166–167, 198–199, *IRB:* 126–127, 143–145, 149, 157

railroads and *IRA:* 156, 167, 197–198, *IRB:* 58, 59, 64–66, 96–97, 149, 157, *IRPS:* 96–97, 179–191

steel and *IRA:* 168–169

Theodore Roosevelt and *IRPS:* 137, 177–178, 179, 180, 190–191, 192, 194, 200–202

William Howard Taft and *IRPS:* 192, 194

Monroe, James *IRB:* 108

More, Sir Thomas *IRA:* 24

Morgan, J. P. *IRA:* 168 (ill.), *IRB:* **95–105**, 100 (ill.), *IRPS:* 180 (ill.)
  art and *IRB:* 102–103
  character of *IRB:* 97–99
  early life of *IRB:* 96–97
  finance and *IRA:* 167–169, *IRB:* 14, 64–66, 95, 96–97, 99–102, 103–104, 157, 191
  John D. Rockefeller and *IRB:* 95, 104
  muckrakers and *IRB:* 121
  philanthropy of *IRB:* 102–103

radio and *IRB:* 191

railroads and *IRB:* 64–66, 96–97, 157, *IRPS:* 179, 180, 183–186, 189

as robber baron *IRA:* 4

steel and *IRA:* 164, *IRB:* 14, 66, 101, 104, *IRPS:* 44

wealth of *IRB:* 48

Morgan, John *IRB:* 179

Morgan, Junius Spencer *IRA:* 168, *IRB:* 96

Morland, Samuel *IRA:* 44

Morse, Samuel F. B. *IRA:* 117 (ill.), *IRB:* 106 (ill.), **106–112**
  early life of *IRB:* 107–108
  Morse Code and *IRA:* 118–120, *IRB:* 10, 106–107, 108–109, *IRPS:* 77
  telegraph and *IRA:* 117–120, *IRB:* 106–107, 108–112, *IRPS:* 46, 75–78, 79–80, 82–83

Morse Code *IRA:* 118 (ill.), *IRPS:* 76 (ill.)
  Andrew Carnegie and *IRB:* 10
  first demonstration of *IRA:* 119–120, *IRB:* 110
  invention of *IRB:* 10, 105, 108–109, *IRPS:* 77
  Thomas Alva Edison and *IRA:* 124

Motors. *See* Engines

Movies *IRA:* 133

Muckrakers. *See also specific muckrakers*
  biographies of *IRB:* 117–128
  definition of *IRA:* 144
  excerpt from *IRPS:* 135–145
  factory system and *IRPS:* 158
  overview of *IRA:* 162–163, *IRB:* 114–116
  Theodore Roosevelt and *IRB:* 157, 158–159
  trusts and *IRB:* 156

Muhammad *IRA:* 220

Muskets. *See* Rifles

Mussolini, Benito *IRB:* 125
My Life and Work *IRB:* 17–18

N

Napoléon I
  economy and *IRA:* 95,
    IRPS: 65–66
  food preservation and
    IRA: 137
  French Revolution and
    IRA: 97, 209
  James J. Hill and *IRB:* 59
  Robert Fulton and *IRB:* 29
National Academy of Design
    IRB: 108
National Equitable Labor
    Exchange *IRB:* 136
National Labor Relations Act
    IRA: 188–189, 203–204
National Labor Relations
    Board *IRA:* 203, *IRB:* 26
Native Americans *IRA:* 112,
    134, 196, *IRB:* 61
Nativist Party *IRB:* 109
Natural gas *IRA:* 121, *IRPS:*
    124
Natural law
  control over *IRA:* 140
  definition of *IRA:* 10
  scientific revolution and
    IRA: 14–16
  socialism and *IRA:* 99,
    100
  society and *IRA:* 20
Nautilus *IRA:* 58
Navigation *IRA:* 14, 20–21,
    27, 56–61. *See also*
    Steamboats
Navigation Acts *IRA:* 27
Networks *IRA:* 154–160,
    IRB: 54–56, *IRPS:* 182
Newcomen, Thomas
  steam engine built by
    IRA: 7, 43–45, 213, *IRPS:*
    48–49, 52
  steam engine improved
    after *IRA:* 45–46, 56,
    IRB: 180, *IRPS:* 52–53
New Deal *IRA:* 179, 202–205
New Harmony *IRA:* 92, *IRB:*
    135–136

**"Newspaper Enterprise—
    Extraordinary Express
    from Lexington, Ken-
    tucky"** *IRPS:* **80–82**
Newspapers *IRPS:* 75–77,
    78–83, 84. *See also* Jour-
    nalism
Newton, Sir Isaac *IRA:* 15,
    16 (ill.)
New View of Society, A *IRB:*
    134–135
New York Central Railroad
    IRA: 159
New York Evening Post *IRB:*
    123
New York Stock Exchange
    IRB: 61, 62 (ill.). *See also*
    Stock market
New York Times *IRPS:* 113,
    115
New York Tribune *IRB:* 117
New York Volkszeitung *IRPS:*
    112
Nitroglycerine *IRA:* 131
Nobel, Alfred *IRA:* 131
Northern Pacific Railroad
  building of *IRB:* 61, 63
  monopolies and *IRA:*
    197–198, *IRB:* 64–66,
    157, *IRPS:* 179, 183–186
***Northern Securities Co.* v.
    United States *IRPS:*
    179–191**
**Northern Securities Com-
    pany** *IRA:* 197–198,
    IRB: 65–66, 157, *IRPS:*
    179–191
Nuclear power *IRA:* 213

O

Oil *IRA:* 221 (ill.), *IRB:* 141
    (ill.). *See also* Gas; Gaso-
    line
  business of *IRB:* 143
  competition and *IRB:* 116
  discovery of *IRA:*
    112–113, 165, *IRB:*
    141–142
  finance and *IRA:* 165, 166
  impact of *IRB:* 142

internal combustion en-
    gine and *IRA:* 1, 3, 113
John D. Rockefeller and
    IRB: 116, 125–126, 139,
    142–144
Middle East and *IRA:*
    220–221
monopolies and *IRA:* 163,
    166–167, 198–199, *IRB:*
    126–127, 139, 143–145,
    149, 157
muckrakers and *IRA:* 163
transportation and *IRA:* 3,
    151
Oldsmobile *IRA:* 148
On Ministerial Plan of Reform
    IRPS: 106
On Poor Laws for Ireland
    IRPS: 106
*On the Distress of the Agricul-
    tural Labourers* *IRPS:*
    106
Otto, Nikolaus *IRA:* 115
Ottoman Empire *IRA:* 220
Out of Mulberry Street *IRB:*
    118
Outram, Benjamin *IRA:* 53
Owen, Caroline (Dale) *IRB:*
    132
Owen, Robert *IRA:* 91–93,
    IRB: 130 (ill.), **130–137**
Owen, William *IRB:* 135,
    136

P

Pacific Railway Act *IRB:* 60
Paint *IRA:* 166, *IRB:* 3–4
Panama Canal *IRB:* 56
Panic of 1907 *IRB:* 193–194
Papin, Denis *IRA:* 44, 56
Parliament *IRA:* 87 (ill.),
    IRPS: 102 (ill.)
  Chartists and *IRA:* 97–98,
    IRPS: 13
  Combination Acts *IRA:*
    103
  Factory Act of 1833 *IRA:*
    90–91, *IRPS:* 110
  Frame Breaking Act *IRA:*
    94–95, *IRPS:* 73

Gagging Acts *IRA:* 98, 103–104

Reform Bill of 1832 *IRA:* 86–89, *IRPS:* 14

Robert Owen and *IRB:* 134

Sadler Report and *IRPS:* 101, 106, 110

tariffs and *IRA:* 194

Pasteur, Louis *IRB:* 126

Patents

brakes and *IRB:* 185, 186

canals and *IRB:* 31

cotton gin and *IRA:* 74, *IRB:* 199–200, 201

function of *IRB:* 3, 200, *IRPS:* 48

generators and *IRB:* 184, 189

George Westinghouse and *IRA:* 126, *IRB:* 186, 187, 192, 194

government regulation of *IRPS:* 199

internal combustion engine and *IRA:* 114

Nikola Tesla and *IRA:* 126, *IRB:* 185, 194

reapers and *IRA:* 136, *IRB:* 90

refrigeration and *IRA:* 139

Robert McCormick and *IRB:* 90

spinning machines and *IRA:* 69, 72

steamboats and *IRA:* 56, *IRB:* 34

steam engines and *IRA:* 38–39, 42, *IRB:* 181, *IRPS:* 45, 48, 49, 52, 53

steel and *IRA:* 129–130

telegraph and *IRA:* 124, *IRB:* 110, 111, *IRPS:* 78

telephones and *IRA:* 120

Thomas Alva Edison and *IRA:* 123

Paul, Lewis *IRA:* 69

Peabody, George *IRB:* 96

Peasants *IRA:* 2 (ill.), 13, 96

Peel, Robert (elder) *IRB:* 134

Peel, Robert (younger) *IRB:* 134

Pennsylvania Railroad *IRA:* 160–161, *IRB:* 10–11, 55–56

Pensions *IRA:* 172, 188, 189–190, *IRB:* 15, *IRPS:* 42

Percival, Thomas *IRB:* 132

Perry, Matthew C. *IRA:* 217, 217 (ill.)

Petroleum. *See* Oil

Philanthropy

Andrew Carnegie and *IRA:* 164–165, *IRB:* 14–15, 53, 102, *IRPS:* 35, 40–43, 148

Jay Gould and *IRB:* 53

John D. Rockefeller and *IRB:* 53, 139, 144–146

J. P. Morgan and *IRB:* 102–103

Samuel F. B. Morse and *IRB:* 112

Philippines *IRA:* 219

Phillips, David Graham *IRA:* 162

The Philosophy of Manufactures *IRPS:* 13–20

Physics *IRA:* 34

Physiocrats *IRA:* 29, *IRB:* 164

Pin making *IRPS:* 3–4, 6–7

Pistons

definition of *IRA:* 36, 75

development of *IRA:* 41

operation of *IRA:* 37, 43, 45–47, 113, *IRB:* 18, 19, *IRPS:* 48–49

steam locomotives and *IRA:* 53–54

Plastics *IRA:* 132–133

Platt, Thomas *IRB:* 77

Plows *IRA:* 135–136, *IRB:* 89, 92, *IRPS:* 87

Politics *IRPS:* 147, 148. *See also* Government; *specific political parties*

Polo, Marco *IRA:* 218

Poor Laws *IRA:* 194

Population *IRA:* 83–84, 108–109, 214, 220. *See also* Urbanization

Potter, Beatrice *IRPS:* 153

Poverty

agriculture and *IRA:* 175, *IRB:* 70

factory system and *IRA:* 96, 172–175, *IRB:* 69–70, 71

government and *IRA:* 194, 199–205, *IRPS:* 43–44

inequality of *IRB:* 72

muckrakers and *IRA:* 162, 163, *IRB:* 114–115, 116, 117–119, 120–121

social work and *IRA:* 172, 191–192, *IRPS:* 146–154

urbanization and *IRA:* 84

Prices *IRB:* 18

Priestly, Joseph *IRA:* 48

Princeton University *IRB:* 15

"Principles of Population" *IRA:* 83–84

The Principles of Scientific Management *IRA:* 152

Printing press *IRA:* 16–17, 18 (ill.), *IRB:* 2

Productivity. *See also* Efficiency

agriculture and *IRA:* 3, 5, 25–26, 73–74, 83–84, 134–136, 214, *IRB:* 93

automobiles and *IRB:* 22–23, 27

cotton gin and *IRA:* 73–74

factory system and *IRA:* 76–78, 146, *IRPS:* 13–14, 19, 54–61, 63

hours and *IRPS:* 104

industrialization and *IRA:* 4

labor and *IRPS:* 54–61, 63

specialization and *IRPS:* 3–4, 6–11

steam engines and *IRA:* 41–42, 44–45, *IRPS:* 50–51

steel and *IRB:* 6

textiles and *IRA:* 67, 71, 75, 76–78, 93, 112, *IRB:* 9, 131, *IRPS:* 54–61, 63

Progress *IRA:* 6–7, 215–216

Progressive Party

muckrakers and *IRB:* 156

platform of *IRPS:*
192–203
Theodore Roosevelt and
IRB: 158, *IRPS:* 158,
177–178, 190, 192–193,
200–203
Proletariat *IRA:* 103, *IRB:* 83,
IRPS: 23, 28–31
Property
Communism and *IRPS:*
39–40
government and *IRA:* 20,
IRPS: 180–181
Marxism and *IRA:* 99,
100–101, *IRPS:* 23,
25–28, 31
Protestantism *IRA:* 17–20
Puffing Billy IRB: 173
Puffing Devil IRB: 172
Pullman, George *IRA:* 180,
181
Pullman strike *IRA:* 180–181
Pumps *IRA:* 7, 39, 41–43

Q

Quadricycle *IRA:* 148, *IRB:*
20, 21 (ill.)

R

Radio *IRB:* 185, 190–192
Railroads *IRA:* 53 (ill.), 133
(ill.), 157 (ill.), *IRB:* 192
(ill.), *IRPS:* 86 (ill.), 91
(ill.). *See also* Steam locomotives
agriculture and *IRA:* 137,
157, *IRB:* 59, 61, 63–64,
IRPS: 87–88
Andrew Carnegie and
IRA: 160–161, *IRB:*
10–12, 55, 56
Baltimore and Ohio Rail-
road *IRB:* 53
brakes and *IRA:* 126, *IRB:*
184, 185–187, 193
Canadian Pacific Railroad
IRB: 62

Central Pacific Railroad
IRB: 63, *IRPS:* 89, 94–96,
97
Chicago, Burlington, and
Quincy Railroad *IRB:*
65, *IRPS:* 183–184
coal and *IRA:* 51–53, 157,
IRB: 60, 171–175
competition and *IRA:*
167, 197–198, *IRB:*
50–51, 55–56, 58–59,
60–67, 96–97, 157,
IRPS: 88–89, 179–189
Darlington Railway *IRB:*
171
Denver and Rio Grande
Railroad *IRB:* 55, 56
development of *IRA:*
50–53, *IRB:* 172–175
electricity and *IRB:* 191
Erie Railroad Company
IRB: 50–51
factory system and *IRA:*
52
finance and *IRA:*
154–155, 159–160, 168,
IRB: 47–48, 49–53,
64–66, 96–97, 157
food and *IRA:* 121
government and *IRA:*
155, 197–198, *IRB:* 58,
59, 60–61, 61–62,
64–66, 157
Great Northern Railroad
IRA: 197–198, *IRB:* 65,
66, 67, 157, *IRPS:* 87,
179, 183–186
growth of *IRA:* 156–160,
IRB: 58–59, 60–64, *IRPS:*
85–97
immigration and *IRB:*
60–61, 63–64, *IRPS:* 87,
89, 93
impact of *IRPS:* 46, 86–89,
96–97
intercontinental *IRB:* 60
International and Great
Northern Railroad *IRB:*
55
iron and *IRA:* 52–53, 157,
161
labor and *IRB:* 64

labor unions and *IRA:*
180–181
Liverpool and Manchester
Railway *IRB:* 174–175
Manhattan Elevated Rail-
road *IRB:* 54
manufacturing and *IRB:*
61
Missouri Pacific Railroad
IRB: 52–53, 55–56
monopolies and *IRA:* 156,
167, 197–198, *IRB:* 58,
59, 64–66, 96–97, 149,
157, *IRPS:* 96–97,
179–191
networks and *IRA:*
154–155, 155–156,
156–160, *IRB:* 54–56,
IRPS: 182
New York Central Railroad
IRA: 159
Northern Pacific Railroad
IRA: 197–198, *IRB:* 61,
63, 64–66, 157, *IRPS:*
179, 183–186
Northern Securities Com-
pany *IRA:* 197–198,
IRB: 65–66, 157, *IRPS:*
179–189
Pennsylvania Railroad
IRA: 160–161, *IRB:*
10–11, 55–56
Pullman strike and *IRA:*
180–181
refrigeration and *IRA:*
139–140
signaling systems for *IRB:*
186–187, 193
Southern Pacific Railroad
IRB: 55, 67, 74
St. Paul and Pacific Railroad *IRB:* 60, 61–64
standardization and *IRA:*
155–156, 158–159
steamboats and *IRB:* 60
steam locomotives and
IRA: 52, 53–56
steel and *IRA:* 130, 163,
IRPS: 96
Stockton and Darlington
Railway *IRA:* 55, *IRB:*
173–174
strikes and *IRA:* 180–181

telegraph and *IRA:* 117, 120, 121, *IRB:* 53, 55, 111, 112, *IRPS:* 88, 89, 93, 95–96

Texas and Pacific Railroad *IRB:* 52, 55

transcontinental *IRPS:* 85–97

transportation and *IRA:* 50–53, 158

trucking and *IRA:* 153–154, 158

Union Pacific Railroad *IRB:* 52, 55, 63, 65, 67, *IRPS:* 89, 93, 94–96

Wabash Railroad *IRB:* 51–52, 55

Western Pacific Railroad *IRB:* 55

Ramsay, David *IRA:* 38–39

Rawfords Mill *IRA:* 94, 95

Rayon *IRA:* 132

Reapers *IRB:* 91 (ill.)
development of *IRA:* 134–135, *IRB:* 88, 90–91
impact of *IRB:* 93, *IRPS:* 87
operation of *IRB:* 89
production of *IRB:* 91–93

Recessions *IRA:* 201 (ill.)
of 1869 *IRB:* 52
of 1873 *IRB:* 61
of 1893 *IRB:* 64–65
of 1907 *IRB:* 193–194
government regulation and *IRA:* 193
Great Depression *IRA:* 199–205, *IRB:* 25, 125
wages and *IRB:* 25

Refining *IRB:* 143

Reform Bill of 1832 *IRA:* 88–89, *IRPS:* 14

Refrigeration *IRA:* 138–140

Regulation. *See* Government regulation

Religion
Enlightenment and *IRA:* 21, 22
God in *IRA:* 13, 14, 19–20
Islam *IRA:* 220–221
John D. Rockefeller and *IRB:* 140
Marxism and *IRB:* 84

Medieval period and *IRA:* 13, 14
printing press and *IRA:* 16–17
Protestantism *IRA:* 17–20
Reformation and *IRA:* 17–20
Robert Owen and *IRA:* 93, *IRB:* 134, 135
Roman Catholic Church *IRA:* 13, 16–17, 17–20, 21
science and *IRA:* 14–15, 18, 19, *IRB:* 135

Renaissance
definition of *IRA:* 10
democracy and *IRA:* 20
England and *IRA:* 40
Enlightenment and *IRA:* 21–22
literacy and *IRA:* 16–17
Middle East and *IRA:* 220
navigation and *IRA:* 14, 20–21
overview of *IRA:* 12–14
progress and *IRA:* 7
Reformation and *IRA:* 17–20
scientific revolution and *IRA:* 13, 14–16, 40, 130–131
steam and *IRA:* 38–41

Republican Party
business and *IRA:* 196, *IRB:* 43, *IRPS:* 195
labor unions and *IRA:* 188, 205
Theodore Roosevelt and *IRPS:* 190

Reuther, Walter *IRB:* 26 (ill.)

Revolution. *See also* Industrial Revolution; Marxism
American Revolution *IRA:* 9, 30, 48, 209
French Revolution *IRA:* 9, 48, 88, 95, 96, 97, 209, *IRB:* 202, *IRPS:* 66
Marxism and *IRA:* 99–103, *IRB:* 79–80, 81–82, 84, *IRPS:* 2, 21–22, 23, 29–32
Mexican Revolution *IRB:* 124

Revolution of 1848 *IRB:* 81–82, *IRPS:* 23, 32

Russian Revolution *IRA:* 9, 101, 203

scientific *IRA:* 13, 14–16, 40, 130–131

socialism and *IRA:* 96–97

Revolution of 1848 *IRB:* 81–82, *IRPS:* 23, 32

Reynolds, Richard *IRA:* 53

Rheinische Zeitung IRB: 81

Rifles *IRB:* 197, 202–204

Riis, Caroline *IRB:* 117

Riis, Elizabeth (Nielsen) *IRB:* 118

Riis, Jacob *IRA:* 162, *IRB:* 114, 116, 117 (ill.), **117–119**, 156

Riis, Mary (Phillips) *IRB:* 118

Riis, Niels Edward *IRB:* 117

Roads *IRPS:* 199

Robber barons. See also *specific robber barons*
definition of *IRA:* 4, 144, *IRB:* 47
influence of *IRA:* 160
muckrakers and *IRB:* 156
railroads and *IRA:* 157

Robert Fulton: Engineer and Artist IRB: 32–33

Robert Stephenson and Company *IRB:* 174–175

Robison, John *IRA:* 45

Rockefeller, Eliza *IRB:* 140

Rockefeller, John D. *IRA:* 166 (ill.), *IRB:* 139 (ill.)
coal and *IRB:* 75, 76
early life of *IRB:* 140–141
J. P. Morgan and *IRA:* 169, *IRB:* 95, 104
Mother Jones and *IRB:* 75, 76
muckrakers and *IRB:* 114, 116, 125, 126–127
oil and *IRA:* 165–167, 198–199, *IRB:* 116, 125–126, 139, 142–144, *IRPS:* 191
philanthropy of *IRB:* 53, 139, 144–146
as robber baron *IRA:* 4

Rockefeller, Laura Celestia (Spellman) *IRB:* 140
Rockefeller, William *IRB:* 140, 142
Rockefeller Foundation *IRB:* 146
Rockefeller Institute for Medical Research *IRB:* 145–146
Rocket IRB: 174 (ill.), 175
Rods *IRA:* 36, 37, 41, 113, *IRB:* 18
Roebuck, John *IRB:* 181
Rogers, Will *IRB:* 27
Roman Catholic Church *IRA:* 13, 16–17, 17–20, 21
Roman Empire *IRA:* 12–13
Röntgen, Wilhelm Conrad *IRB:* 191
Roosevelt, Alice Hathaway (Lee) *IRB:* 150
Roosevelt, Alice Lee *IRB:* 150
Roosevelt, Franklin Delano *IRA:* 163, 179, 193, 202–205
Roosevelt, Martha (Bulloch) *IRB:* 149
Roosevelt, Theodore *IRA:* 198 (ill.), *IRB:* **148–159**, 148 (ill.), 151 (ill.), 153 (ill.), *IRPS:* **192–203**,195 (ill.), 201 (ill.)
   coal and *IRB:* 154–155
   early life of *IRB:* 149–150
   government regulation and *IRPS:* 158, 182, 190
   monopolies and *IRA:* 167, 197–199, *IRB:* 58, 59, 66, 139, 148–149, 155–158, *IRPS:* 137, 177–178, 179, 180, 190–191
   Mother Jones and *IRA:* 184, *IRB:* 76–77
   muckrakers and *IRA:* 162, 163, *IRB:* 114, 118, 120, 123, 157, 158–159, *IRPS:* 135
   political career of *IRB:* 150–159
   Progressive Party and *IRB:* 158, *IRPS:* 158, 177–178, 190, 192–193, 200–203

Rough Riders *IRB:* 148, 150, 151 (ill.), 152
Rousseau, Jean-Jacques *IRA:* 21
Rubber *IRA:* 132
Rue, Thomas de la *IRB:* 3
Rumsey, James *IRA:* 57
Russia. *See also* Union of Soviet Socialist Republics
   Japan and *IRA:* 217–218
Russian Revolution *IRA:* 9, 101, 203, *IRB:* 79, 124, *IRPS:* 21–22, 32
Russo-Japanese War *IRA:* 217–218

S

Sacco, Nicola *IRB:* 121
Sadler, Michael *IRA:* 89–90, 93, *IRPS:* 13, **101–110**
Sadler Report *IRA:* 89–90, *IRPS:* 13, **101–109**
Sales *IRPS:* 49
Salt *IRA:* 139
Sapiro, Aaron *IRB:* 25
Saudi Arabia *IRA:* 220
Savannah IRA: 60–61, *IRB:* 35
Savery, Thomas *IRA:* 42–43, *IRB:* 180, *IRPS:* 45, **47–53**
Schwab, Charles *IRB:* 12, 101
Science
   chemistry and *IRA:* 130–133
   empiricism of *IRA:* 10, 15, 22, 48
   energy and *IRA:* 34
   industrialization and *IRA:* 210
   instruments for *IRB:* 178–180
   Lunar Society and *IRA:* 48
   management and *IRA:* 152–153
   metallurgy and *IRA:* 127–130
   religion and *IRA:* 14–15, 18, 19, *IRB:* 135

Renaissance and *IRA:* 13, 14–16, 40, 130–131
Scott, Thomas A. *IRB:* 10
Scythes *IRA:* 135, *IRB:* 89, 90
Service economy *IRA:* 210, 214–215
Seven Years War *IRA:* 23, 30
The Shame of the Cities IRB: 124
Shay, Michael *IRPS:* 93
Shepherd, William G. *IRPS:* **156–163**
Sherman Antitrust Act. *See also* Monopolies
   description of *IRB:* 144–145
   oil and *IRA:* 163, 167, 198–199, *IRB:* 127, 157
   Progressive Party and *IRPS:* 202
   railroads and *IRA:* 197–198, *IRB:* 66, 157, *IRPS:* 97, 179–181, 185–189
Shipping. *See* Navigation
Shirley, a Tale IRPS: **65**, 69–73
Shock absorbers *IRB:* 194
Signaling systems *IRB:* 186–187, 192 (ill.), 193
Sinclair, Guinevere Jeanne *IRB:* 57
Sinclair, Meta (Fuller) *IRB:* 120
Sinclair, Upton *IRB:* 120 (ill.), *IRPS:* **135–145**, 139 (ill.)
   livestock and *IRA:* 163, *IRB:* 116, **119–122**
   muckraking by *IRB:* 114, 119–122, 156
Slater, Samuel *IRA:* 109–110, 110 (ill.), 192
Slavery *IRA:* 65 (ill.), *IRB:* 202 (ill.)
   cotton gin and *IRA:* 64, 74, *IRB:* 196, 199, 201
   labor and *IRB:* 120, *IRPS:* 104, 122
   Mother Jones and *IRB:* 71
   political division over *IRA:* 108–109

Robert McCormick and
IRB: 89

Small, William *IRA:* 48

Smart, Peter *IRPS:* 103–107

Smith, Adam *IRA:* 193 (ill.),
IRB: 161 (ill.), **161–168,**
IRPS: 4 (ill.), **1–12**
capitalism of *IRA:* 29, *IRB:*
161–162
competition and *IRB:*
156, 165–166
death of *IRB:* 168
early life of *IRB:* 162–164,
IRPS: 5
government regulation
and *IRA:* 192, *IRB:*
166–167, *IRPS:* 1–2
James Watt and *IRPS:* 12
Karl Marx and *IRPS:* 32
mercantilism and *IRA:* 10,
30, *IRB:* 164–165
specialization and *IRPS:*
3–11

Smith, Adam (economist's
father) *IRPS:* 5

Smith, Margaret (Douglas)
IRPS: 5

Sobrero, Ascanio *IRA:* 131

Socialism. *See also* Communism; Marxism
Chartists and *IRA:* 97–98
communism and *IRPS:* 32
competition and *IRB:*
144, 153–154
cottage industries and
IRPS: 36–37
definition of *IRA:* 84, 172
Eugene Debs and *IRPS:*
193
Franklin D. Roosevelt and
IRA: 204–205
Henry Ford and *IRB:* 23
labor and *IRA:* 96–97,
176, 179–182, 184, 186,
190, *IRB:* 23, 37, 39–40,
43, 44, 45, 130,
132–136, *IRPS:* 62
Marxism and *IRA:* 99–103
Robert Owen and *IRB:*
130, 132–136
Upton Sinclair and *IRB:*
116, 121
war and *IRB:* 44

wealth and *IRA:* 96–97,
IRPS: 34–35, 38–40

Social reform *IRA:* 91–93,
IRB: 23–24, 117–119,
133–136, 161–162

Social security *IRA:* 193, 203

Social work *IRA:* 172,
191–192, *IRPS:* 146–155

Society
automobiles and *IRA:*
116, 151–154, 158
corporations and *IRPS:*
198
factory system and *IRA:* 2,
3–6, 64–66, 78–81,
83–86, 171–175, *IRB:*
133–136
Great Depression and
IRA: 199–205
immigration and *IRA:* 199
Luddites and *IRA:* 95
manufacturing and *IRA:*
213–215, *IRPS:* 37
Marxism and *IRA:*
102–103
natural law and *IRA:* 20
progress and *IRA:* 6–7
Progressive Party and
IRPS: 192–203
standardization and *IRA:*
223
steam locomotives and
IRA: 55–56
textiles and *IRA:* 64–66,
78–81
wealth and *IRA:* 4,
164–165, *IRPS:* 34–42

Somerset, Edward *IRA:*
39–40, 41–42

Sorocold, George *IRPS:* 50

South America *IRA:*
222–223

South Brooklyn News IRB:
117

"South Carolina Exposition
and Protest" *IRA:* 195

Southern Pacific Railroad
IRB: 55, 67, 74

Soviet Union *IRB:* 80, 125,
IRPS: 21–22. *See also*
Russia

Spain *IRA:* 222

Spanish-American War *IRB:*
148, 151–152

Specialization *IRA:* 78–79,
146, *IRPS:* 3–11

Spinning *IRA:* 70 (ill.), 71
(ill.), *IRPS:* 61 (ill.)
cottage industries and
IRA: 66–67
definition of *IRA:* 28, 64
machines and *IRA:* 67,
69–73, 74–75,. 109–110,
IRPS: 16–17, 108
process of *IRA:* 68

Spinning jenny *IRA:* 69–73

Spinning mule *IRA:* 72–73,
74, *IRB:* 131

Spinning wheel *IRPS:* 61
(ill.)

St. Paul and Pacific Railroad
IRB: 60, 61–64

Stalin, Joseph *IRB:* 125

Stamps *IRB:* 2–3

Standardization
education and *IRA:* 223
food and *IRA:* 223
interchangeable parts and
IRA: 4, 80–81, 144,
145–146, 146–147, 223
networks and *IRA:*
155–156
of people *IRA:* 223
railroads and *IRA:*
155–156, 158–159

Standard Oil Company. *See
also* Standard Oil Trust
domination by *IRA:* 198,
IRB: 139, 142–144
formation of *IRA:* 166
muckrakers and *IRB:* 116,
123, 125, 126–127

Standard Oil Trust. *See also*
Standard Oil Company
breakup of *IRA:* 198–199,
IRB: 139, 143–144, 157,
IRPS: 191
growth of *IRA:* 165–167
muckrakers and *IRA:* 163,
IRB: 127

Stanford, Leland *IRPS:* 89,
94, 95

Stanley, William *IRB:* 193

Starr, Ellen *IRA:* 191–192,
IRPS: 146, 147, 148, 152

The State and Prospects of the Country IRPS: 106

States' rights IRPS: 188–189, 196, 200–201

Steam IRA: 16, 34–41, 116, IRB: 180. See also *specific technologies*

Steamboats IRB: 33 (ill.). *See also* Navigation
development of IRA: 56–61, IRB: 32–34
impact of IRA: 158, IRB: 29–30, 34–35
railroads and IRB: 60

Steam engines IRA: 11 (ill.)
coal and IRA: 1, 3, 7, 41–43, 45, 47, 49, 111–112, 213, IRB: 19, 177, 180, 181, IRPS: 45, 47–48, 51–52, 123
development of IRA: 1, 7, 11–12, 16, 38–41, 42–47, 213, IRB: 32, 177, 180–183, IRPS: 45, 47–53
energy and IRA: 35
finance and IRA: 44
iron and IRA: 45
labor and IRPS: 18
operation of IRA: 3, 36–37, 113, 116, IRB: 18, IRPS: 47–49, 51–52
patents and IRA: 38–39, 42
productivity and IRA: 41–42, 44–45
pumps and IRA: 7, 39, 41–43
steamboats and IRA: 56–61
textiles and IRA: 72, 75–76, 109, 112, IRB: 181–182
tractors and IRA: 136
transportation and IRA: 3, 50
uses for IRPS: 49–52

Steam locomotives IRA: 53 (ill.), IRB: 174 (ill.). *See also* Railroads
coal and IRA: 52
development of IRA: 52, 53–55, IRB: 169, 171–175, IRPS: 91–92

impact of IRA: 55–56, 158

Steel IRA: 131 (ill.). *See also* Iron
Andrew Carnegie and IRA: 161–164, 168, IRB: 1, 8, 11–14, 66, 99, 101, 104, IRPS: 44
coal and IRA: 52, 161
competition and IRA: 168–169
construction and IRA: 163
factory system and IRA: 130
finance and IRA: 168–169, IRB: 14, 66, 101, 104
government and IRB: 66
iron and IRA: 127–130
labor and IRB: 12, 13
monopolies and IRA: 168–169
patents and IRA: 129–130
plows and IRA: 135
production of IRA: 127–130, 161, IRB: 1, 4–6
properties of IRB: 5, 6
railroads and IRA: 130, 163, IRPS: 96
strikes and IRA: 161–163
tariffs and IRA: 194
transportation and IRA: 130

Steffens, Josephine (Bontecou) IRB: 122–123

Steffens, Lincoln IRB: 114, 116, **122–125**, 123 (ill.), 156

Stephens, Uriah IRA: 179

Stephenson, Frances (Henderson) IRB: 170

Stephenson, George IRA: 55, IRB: 169 (ill.), **169–175**

Stephenson, Robert IRA: 55, IRB: 170–171, 172–173, 174–175

Stillman, J. D. B. IRPS: **85–97**, 87 (ill.)

Stockholders IRB: 24, 52, 100. *See also* Corporations

Stock market IRB: 62 (ill.). *See also* Wall Street
brokerage houses and IRB: 48
crash of IRA: 199–203
finance and IRA: 168
panic of 1873 and IRB: 61
panic of 1907 and IRB: 97, 102, 193–194
regulation of IRPS: 200, 202
telegraph and IRA: 124, IRB: 111, 112

Stockton and Darlington Railway IRA: 55, IRB: 173–174

Strasser, Adolph IRB: 40–41

Strikebreakers IRA: 172, 178–179, 186–187

Strikes
Andrew Carnegie and IRA: 161–163
Chartists and IRA: 98
coal and IRA: 186–187, IRB: 74–76, 154–155
definition of IRA: 172, 178
early examples of IRA: 92
Haymarket Square Riot and IRA: 179–182
Homestead Strike IRA: 161–163, IRB: 12, 13
hours and IRA: 179, 182, 187
Knights of Labor and IRA: 179–182
Lawrence Textile Strike of 1912 IRPS: 164–166, 166–168, 174–175, 203
Pullman Strike IRA: 180–181
railroads and IRA: 180–181
regulation of IRA: 188–189, 203–204, 205
steel and IRA: 161–163
strikebreakers and IRA: 172, 178–179, 186–187
violence and IRA: 162–163, 179–183, 186–187
wages and IRA: 161–163, 180–181, IRPS: 164–166, 166–168, 174–175

Strutt, Jedediah *IRA:* 109
Sturgeon, William *IRA:* 118
Submarines *IRA:* 58, *IRB:* 32
Sullivan, Michael *IRPS:* 93
Sutherland, J. B. *IRA:* 139
Swan, Joseph *IRA:* 125
Swedenborg, Emanuel *IRPS:* 39–40
Symington, William *IRA:* 56

T

Taft, Robert *IRA:* 188–189
Taft, William Howard *IRPS:* 190 (ill.)
  business and *IRB:* 158, *IRPS:* 190
  defeat of *IRPS:* 202–203
  election of *IRA:* 186
  labor and *IRB:* 43–44, *IRPS:* 194
  Mother Jones and *IRB:* 74
  nomination of *IRPS:* 192–193
Taft-Hartley Act *IRA:* 188–189, 205
Tarbell, Franklin *IRB:* 125
Tarbell, Ida *IRB:* **125–128**, 126 (ill.), *IRPS:* 136 (ill.)
  early life of *IRB:* 125–126
  feminism and *IRB:* 127–128
  muckraking by *IRA:* 163, 167, *IRB:* 114, 116, 123, 126–127, 156
Tariffs *IRA:* 109, 172, 193–196. *See also* Taxes
Taxes *IRA:* 196–197, *IRPS:* 35, 43, 199. *See also* Tariffs
Taylor, Frederick *IRA:* 151 (ill.), 152–153
Technology *IRA:* 3, *IRPS:* 45–46, 73–74, 133. See *also specific technologies*
Telegraph *IRA:* 115 (ill.), 117 (ill.), 118 (ill.), *IRB:* 106 (ill.), 111 (ill.), *IRPS:* 76 (ill.), 81 (ill.)
  American Civil War and *IRB:* 11

  Andrew Carnegie and *IRB:* 10
  development of *IRA:* 117–120, *IRB:* 106–107, 108–109, *IRPS:* 75–78, 82–83
  electricity and *IRA:* 116–117, 118–119, *IRB:* 108–109, *IRPS:* 77, 79
  factory system and *IRA:* 117, 121
  finance and *IRA:* 120, *IRB:* 106, 107, 109–110, *IRPS:* 76, 77, 78, 82–83, 84
  government and *IRB:* 106, 107, 109–110, *IRPS:* 76, 77, 78, 82–83
  growth of *IRA:* 120, *IRB:* 110–112, *IRPS:* 79–84
  impact of *IRA:* 121–122, *IRB:* 112, *IRPS:* 46, 75–84
  networks and *IRA:* 154, 155
  operation of *IRPS:* 77
  patents and *IRA:* 124, *IRPS:* 78
  railroads and *IRA:* 117, 120, 121, *IRB:* 53, 55, 111, 112, *IRPS:* 88, 89, 93, 95–96
  Thomas Alva Edison and *IRA:* 124
  transportation and *IRA:* 117, 120, 121
Telephones *IRA:* 119 (ill.)
  impact of *IRA:* 117
  invention of *IRA:* 120–122, *IRPS:* 83
  standardization and *IRA:* 155, 156
  telegraph and *IRB:* 55
"Tenement-House Cigar Manufacture" *IRPS:* **112–122**
Tennessee Valley Authority *IRA:* 202–203
Teoli, Camella *IRPS:* **164–175**
Tesla, Nikola *IRA:* 126 (ill.), *IRB:* **184–194**, 188 (ill.)
  awards of *IRA:* 127

  character of *IRB:* 187–188
  death of *IRB:* 194
  electricity and *IRA:* 125–127, *IRB:* 184–185, 188–189
  inventions of *IRB:* 184–185, 189–192
Tesla coil *IRB:* 185, 190
Texas and Pacific Railroad *IRB:* 52, 55
Textiles *IRA:*80 (ill.), 90 (ill.), 111 (ill.), *IRPS:*165 (ill.), 170 (ill.). *See also* Spinning; Weaving
  agriculture and *IRA:*63, 66, 108–109, 222
  Asia and *IRA:*219
  children and *IRA:*63, 65, 77, 79–80, 89–91, 219
  clothmaking process *IRA:*67–69
  competition and *IRA:*93–96, *IRPS:*56, 59–61
  cottage industries and *IRA:*28–29, 63, 66–67, 78, *IRB:*9, *IRPS:*54, 102
  cotton and *IRA:*66, 67
  cotton gin and *IRB:*201–202
  dangers of *IRA:*173, *IRPS:*156–163
  definition of *IRA:*64
  dyes for *IRA:*131
  enclosure movement and *IRA:*66–67, 76, 79
  factory system and *IRA:*63–66, 76–78, 90–91, 192, 219, 222, *IRB:*9, 76–77, 132, *IRPS:*54–62, 63–74, 102, 156–163, 164–175, 203
  government regulation and *IRA:*109–110
  labor and *IRA:*93–96, *IRPS:*54–59, 61–62, 63–74, 101–110, 164–175
  Luddites and *IRA:*93–96
  mechanization of *IRA:*1, 63–66, 67–76, 109–111, *IRPS:*16–17, 54–62, 108

Mother Jones and
IRA:184
productivity and IRA:67,
71, 75, 76–78, 93, 112,
IRB:9, 131, IRPS:54–61,
63
society and IRA:64–66,
78–81
specialization and
IRA:78–79
steam engines and
IRA:72, 75–76, 109,
112, IRB:181–182
tariffs and IRA: 194–196
wages and IRA: 79, 80
water and IRA: 72, 75, 76,
109, 110
wool and IRA: 66, 67
"Texts of the Notting-
hamshire Luddites"
IRA: 94
The Theory of Moral Senti-
ments IRB: 163, 167
Thoreau, Henry David IRA:
81
Time IRA: 6–7, 215, IRPS: 88
Tin Lizzie IRB: 24
Tires IRA: 132
Torpedoes IRA: 59–60
Toynbee, Arnold IRA: 11
Toynbee Hall IRPS: 148
Toynbee House IRA: 191
Tractors IRA: 136, IRB: 89
Trade IRA: 217, 218. See also
Colonialism; Mercantil-
ism
Trade unions. See Labor
unions
Trains. See Railroads
Transportation. See also Automobiles; Navigation;
Railroads; Trucking
agriculture and IRA: 137,
157
automobiles and IRA:
151, 158
energy and IRA: 34
impact of IRPS: 45–46
oil and IRA: 3, 151, IRB:
143
overview of IRA: 3, 158
railroads and IRA: 50–53,
158, IRPS: 85–89, 96–97

steamboats and IRA:
56–61, 158, IRB: 34–35
steam engines and IRA: 3,
50, 158
steam locomotives and
IRA: 52, 53–56, 158
steel and IRA: 130
telegraph and IRA: 117,
120, 121
trucking and IRA:
153–154, 158
A Treatise on the Improvement
of Canal Navigation IRA:
58, IRB: 31
Trevithick, Richard IRA:
53–54, IRB: 172–173
Triangle Shirtwaist Compa-
ny IRA: 173, 174 (ill.),
IRPS: 156–163, 157
(ill.), 159 (ill.), 162 (ill.)
Trotsky, Leon IRB: 124
Trucking IRA: 153–154, 158
Truman, Harry IRA: 190,
205, IRPS: 203
Trusts. See Monopolies
Tull, Jethro IRA: 25
Turney, Hop IRPS: 83
Tuskegee Institute IRA: 164,
IRB: 15, IRPS: 42
Twenty Years at Hull-House
IRA: 191–192, IRPS:
146–155
Two Treatises on Government
IRA: 20

U

Unemployment IRPS:
54–59, 61–62, 66, 68
Union of Soviet Socialist Re-
publics IRB: 80, 125,
IRPS: 21–22. See also
Russia
Union Pacific Railroad
George Jay Gould and
IRB: 55
James J. Hill and IRB: 63,
65, 67
Jay Gould and IRB: 52
"Last Tie" and IRPS: 89,
93, 94–96
Unions. See Labor unions

United Automobile Workers
Union IRB: 17, 25–27
United Mine Workers Union
John L. Lewis and IRA:
186–188
Mother Jones and IRA:
184, IRB: 73, 74
pensions and IRA:
189–190
Theodore Roosevelt and
IRB: 154–155
United Press IRPS: 156
United States of America
IRPS: 22
coal in IRA: 52, 112
individualism in IRA:
176, IRB: 17
industrial revolution in
IRA: 1, 110–111,
171–175, IRB: 39
oil and IRA: 112–113, 151
population in IRA:
108–109, 214
service economy in IRA:
214–215
steamboats in IRA: 57,
60–61
tariffs and IRA: 109,
194–196
textiles in IRA: 108–111
urbanization in IRA: 171
United States Steel IRA: 168,
IRB: 14, 99, 101, IRPS:
44
University of Chicago IRB:
145
Urbanization IRA: 211 (ill.).
See also Enclosure
movement
agriculture and IRA: 134,
210, 213–214, 219
enclosure movement and
IRA: 23–24
factory system and IRA:
5–6, 64, 83–84, 171,
IRPS: 23
food and IRA: 83–84
poverty and IRA: 84
Ure, Andrew IRPS: **13–19**
U.S. Congress
Adamson Act IRB: 44
Clayton Antitrust Act
IRA: 197, IRB: 44